The Belonging Place

he Five Stages Toward Creating an Interdependent Community

By: Janelle Dill

TABLE OF CONTENTS

Kudos

This book is a labor of love. It has taken me years to write down everything I hoped to express into an informative, interactive book. I didn't want to bog down readers with technical jargon or bore them with too much medical information. Throughout the process, I con contacted a number of people I've met over the last few years—with the exception of my older brother, Adam—and asked them to take part in this experiment. I received some confused looks, but I accomplished what I set out to do: write about disabilities and how to better connect as a community. There will always be room for progress! I hope this book will help bridge the gap between the disabled and the able-bodied. I would not have been able to write this without the help of those who wanted to share their stories with the world.

I say kudos to all these incredible individuals who have enriched the world in big or small ways: Kathryn Cagle, Christian Welch, Victims and Villains, Inam Shaleati, The Knepper Family, my older brother, Adam—my dearest brother and friend. Thanks to the Cook family for their contributions to the class work. Special thanks to Tiffany Kairos for her dedication to epilepsy awareness; you are a big help and wonderful friend. Thanks to Formerly Bodies for their beautiful work and the songs they write. Each of these people has put a piece of themselves out there to help shape the world.

Thanks to my support staff—Mom, Dad, sis, and my brother—love you guys! Thanks to my best friend, Brittany Hartman, for not giving up on my dream and for always believing it would happen. Thanks to the Olshefski family for letting me write about disability life on your blog and sharing my story. Thanks for taking the time to hear my ideas—even if they sometimes sound a little "out there." Thanks to Sarah McConahy for editing this magnum opus. I appreciate your candor and fixing the little details. Thanks to anyone who took a few minutes to listen—whether at church or at the dentist's office—thanks for your patience and time. And thanks to you, the reader. This is for you, and I hope you will be touched by what you read. This is dedicated to all my friends who have a disability. Though some of you are far away, I hope you know you are not alone on this journey. I hope you share this book with others and start your own class. It would be an honor for me to help you start your own educational class. If you want my notes, please look in the back of the book for more information.

Introduction

Interdependence (v): inter- inside one + dependence- as one unit, cohesive

(1) To rely on one another; to work harmoniously in a communal sense.

(2) To draw in fellowship with one another; to walk alongside those who are different from each other.

The first time I encountered a disability was through my older brother, Adam; he has autism. I was only three years old, but I knew he was different from other children. He played with his toys in an odd manner. He would flip over his toy truck and spin the wheels, one by one. He would scrunch his eyes closed, and a look that was a cross between a grimace and a grin would spread across his face. Sometimes, my stuff got broken because he would play a little too rough. I remember watching in horror as he once crashed my Barbie car into my dollhouse. As a child, it was difficult to understand.

My mother took us to see our first movie together: Snow White and the Seven Dwarves. She waited until Adam was five years old because she knew he would not be able to sit still long enough without acting up. She sat us down in our seats. My brother's small voice read the words off the screen; "Walt Disney presents: Snow White and the Seven Dwarves." He continued to read the title cards off the screen until the movie began. I didn't see much of the film, though. My seat was hard to sit in, and it sandwiched me like a taco. As the credits scrolled on the screen at the end of the movie, my brother repeatedly bent his knees up and down and read each name aloud, saying, "Stoon, stoon, stoon (a combination of the words "stay tuned"). It bothered me a lot.

"This is stupid," I told my mother. "Why do we have to sit here and watch all these credits? It is completely pointless." My mom rebutted my whining, saying, "Be patient." I didn't want to be patient; I wanted to leave the theater! I didn't understand why my brother had to read all the words off the screen. I was only three at the time. I wanted to be anywhere but in that seat watching those credits.

Over the years, I have learned an incredible thing: if you slow down and choose to be patient, you'll discover hidden treasures that will surprise you. With my brother's penchant for movie credits, I discovered hidden Easter eggs shown only during the credit crawl. How could I, in my immaturity, miss such a wonderful gift?

It turns out I had a lot to discover about the world of disabilities. After my own diagnosis of epilepsy in 2003, I had to adjust my perspective; would I be bitter or better in this difficult time? As I have traversed the highway of disability, I have found five stages of reaching interdependence that need to be experienced by both the disabled and able-bodied: **Fears and Phobias, Scars and Wounds, Obstacles and Barriers, Inclusion and Accommodation, and finally, Belonging and Interdependence**. Not everyone will move through these stages at the same pace. Some may stay stagnant in one phase while others fall back or forward to other stages. There is no solid formula for gaining interdependence. Individuals with and without disabilities in church settings need to rely on one another by listening, talking, and sharing their stories for better solutions to effectively serve as the body of Christ.

Stage One: Addressing the Fears and Phobias That Cause Isolation in Church

God works in our weakness because that's all He has to work with…I should stop seeking happiness in my weakness and start seeking holiness. Pain has a way of purifying my motives and clarifying my calling.

~Clayton King[1]

Remember the reality series from the early 2000s called "Fear Factor?" A contestant had to face their fears by competing in wild—and at times, gross—challenges to win large amounts of money. The challenges ranged from crawling into a box filled with tarantulas to walking on a high wire. Some contestants chickened out; others became sick. But there were the rare few who decided to nip their fears in the bud and go after the money. Viewers thought the contestants were crazy, greedy, brave, or perhaps a combination of all these traits. I think this show was such a hit because people enjoyed watching others face their fears rather than facing their own. Facing a fear head-on is often scary because it takes us outside our comfort zones. We like the warmth of our cocoons where nothing and nobody can shake us. When we are confronted with an ugly thing, we want to fly from it or ignore it.

I had to face my fear of drowning by taking swimming lessons when I was ten. I hated the water. My Pappy D's house had a lake and pond. I loved looking out at the water, but I was terrified of going in. I had fallen in by accident when I was six years old. Twice! It was scary. I was convinced the fish were going to eat me! I know that sounds silly, but that was the truth. I hated not being able to touch the bottom. The pond was so deep that I never knew where to put my feet. Even swimming with a life jacket frightened me. My mom was tired of my excuses to avoid the lake or beach, so she signed up my brother and I for lessons at the local pool. My instructor, Melody, was very kind and helpful. She made sure I didn't fall in or drown. She made swimming seem easy. At thirteen, I went up for baptism at church. For years, I had shrunk back from that, thinking I would sink. Though I'm not the best at swimming (I don't care for it, honestly), I have learned to conquer the paralyzing fear of drowning.

A fear of helplessness or disfiguring madness frequently appears in films, television shows, books, and laws. Early in the silent screen years, a villain had a disfigured face or body to signify wickedness. The hero was portrayed as Adonis-like, with an aquiline nose, well-sculpted chest, and a body free from imperfections. The ugly, disfigured villains were vengeful and angry and often died at the end of the film. There was no room for anyone with a disability. A book called *The Kallikak Family* spawned the fear that those with a disability were a menace to society, including those with a mental illness. In 1918, the United States signed a bill against foreigners, which included anyone with a disability. Disabilities had no place in society; those with disabilities were spurned, isolated, and kept from public view. A person with a disability could be sent to an institution without his or her consent. The fear of a disability still plagues us today. Turn on the news and you'll see the suspect accused of a crime considered "mentally unstable."

In the church, the fear of a disability is more disheartening. A clergyman started the idea of sterilizing the disabled. He thought that keeping the vile, impure disabled from church would lessen the chance of sin. He was wrong; his idea promoted the annihilation of those who had disabilities. This has become known as eugenics. Some churches in the United States have used Leviticus 13-15:15 to

---

[1] Taken from *Stronger: How Hard Times Reveal God's Greatest Power.* 2015, Baker Books.

promote the segregation of those with disabilities. Leviticus 13-15 is well-known for its list of regulations to keep impurities outside the temple and community. For many, this section endorses segregation.

Leviticus 13:45-46 states about leprosy: "The leprous person who has the disease shall wear torn clothes and let the hair of his head hang loose, and he shall cover his upper lip and cry out, "Unclean, unclean." He shall remain unclean as long as he has the disease. He is unclean. He shall live alone. His dwelling shall be outside the camp." (ESV)

Leviticus 21:18-20 goes further to include all sorts of defects. "For no one who has a blemish shall draw near, a man blind or lame, or one who has a mutilated face or a limb too long, or a man who has an injured foot or an injured hand, or a hunchback or a dwarf or a man with a defect in his sight or an itching disease or scabs or crushed loins." (ESV)

Before a few critics say, "I know this sponsored segregation!" I want to point out that the historical context must be kept in mind. In the Ancient Near East, around 4000BC, those who had a disability were not allowed to serve in the larger community. Families with members who had disabilities and individuals with a disability would be placed in a separate community with others like them—i.e., lepers were put with other lepers. The temple priests, like Aaron, had to be careful when entering the temple (see Leviticus 8:31-6 to see the purification process of Aaron and his sons). If he had even one impure thought, God could strike him dead. The priest's laymen would tie a cord around the priest's ankle before he entered the Holy of Holies so they could safely pull him out if he were struck dead by the Almighty.

Leviticus 15 is not about the impurities of the disabled, but rather about the impurities of humanity as a whole. No matter how great our efforts, we cannot get close to the perfection of God on our own merits because God is holy and we are not. God is pure and we are impure. We have fears and phobias. We have flaws. In conversations with my disabled friends, we have discovered that the primary emotion after the diagnosis of a disability is fear. Fear causes isolation when being treated differently from others and judged solely on the basis of your disability. Fear shows up when your disability makes an appearance at a bad time, maybe while driving, at work, or on a date. Fear rears its head when you want to be part of something but because of the limitations of your disability, you feel left out. Fear lashes out in anger at others and at oneself. Fear is a strong motivator toward finding hope or feeling helpless.

The first kind of fear, the fear of those with a disability, comes when a disability is misunderstood or misconstrued. My disability, epilepsy, is often confused with drunkenness or drug addiction. A lot of my able-bodied friends are sometimes afraid to interact with me because they don't know what to do or they are afraid of offending me. It is important for the church to get past this fear and develop vital interactions with those walking in fear. As my brother has taught me, we need to sit down and discuss our fears openly. Share with one another why we are so scared to talk about disabilities. The church body can do that by having classes and support groups. It is vital to educate others about the variety of disabilities in the world.

The other type of fear, the fears of the disability community is a growing problem. The disabled struggle with the fear of people knowing about their disability, being considered weird, and the pressures of ableism. Ableism is a myth perpetuated to create a sense of wholeness, of perfection. It often causes panic among the disability community because it sets an imaginary standard that is often too high to measure up to. The church can address the fears of the disabled by welcoming those who continue to struggle with problems unique to a disability. What is keeping you from addressing fears and phobias? Do you know what your fears and phobias are as a person or in your church? How will you talk about it?

Activity 1: Fears and Phobias

Break into small groups and hand each person a note card. Have everyone write down a fear they have, whether physical or psychological. Have those who are willing to share talk about their fear: how old you were when it first scared you? Why did it scare you? If you are able, share whether or not you have fully faced your fear. Further questions to consider: How did you feel sharing your fears? Did you feel vulnerable? Do you think it can help you connect with someone else who has a disability? Why or why not?

Disability Films

It is important to highlight films that feature characters with a disability. The films I have chosen take major steps toward introducing people to a disability. Whether using humor or a great storyline, these films have a lot to tell us about how we see disabilities—both positively and negatively. A few films I have chosen landmark some firsts—first film to use animators with a disability, first actor with a disability to win an award, etc. In this first section, I have listed films with characters that confront someone with a disability or someone with a disability who confront their fears of rejection and loneliness. For stage one, I have chosen a handful of films for children, teens, adults and families to watch. At the end, there are a few discussion questions. It is best to watch these films in a group or with your family. Some of the material may be difficult to understand or get a little technical, so I advise you to work together, listen, and check out the Disability Films Section in the Appendix.

Some films to introduce a disability to kids & tweens

- Shrek

- Finding Dory

- Frozen

- A Dolphin's Tale

For teens and adults

- Electricity

- Still Alice

- Fifty First Dates

- Garden State

Examine the film. How does it add to or take away from our perceptions of those with a disability??

03/28/2011

Spotlight: Adam Dill, creator of MizAdventures of Evel Janelle Comics, Somerset, PA

I decided to start with my brother, Adam. He was diagnosed with Pervasive Development Disorder at age 2. This is a form of autism that delays development of things like learning to tie one's shoes. Adam has always had a thing for words. Ever since I can remember, he has loved words on screens, tampering with vocabulary, and manipulating logos. He memorizes facts about studio companies that produce television shows and movies. He enjoys developing his own programs and video games. He creates comic strips with goofy characters. His most beloved character developed when we were in high school. That character is Evel Janelle. She was created in 2000, three years before my diagnosis of epilepsy.

He felt terrible when I was diagnosed with epilepsy at nineteen. He thought it was the end of the world! We had to figure out whether or not Evel Janelle would have epilepsy, too. We decided to let her have epilepsy and still represent the lovable, experimental gal who tries hard but fails often. Evel Janelle is based off me. He took some of the goofy things I did growing up and turned it into a series of comic strips. I can't tell you which ones are real and which ones aren't; that is a secret I am not able to disclose.

When my brother is not creating comic strip characters or video game ideas, he volunteers as a shredder at our local hospital. He enjoys music, reading his Bible, watching classic cartoon shows, and playing with cats. If you are interested in seeing his work or the interview I did with him, be sure to look at the Additional Resources/Information page to find the link for his comic strip. There are plenty of pictures there, and I hope the comic strip series will be uploaded soon for everyone to enjoy!

Stage 2: Scars and Wounds - Finding Healing Amidst the Things that Hurt

Compassion is hard because it requires the inner disposition to go with others to places where they are weak, vulnerable, lonely, and broken. But this is not our spontaneous response to suffering. What we desire most is to do away with suffering by fleeing from it or finding a quick cure for it.

~Henri Nouwen, Out of Solitude

Scars are a calling card for great stories. I have plenty of scars from doing some fascinating things—and a few not-so-good things. My most visible scar is my two front teeth. When I was two, I fell off a swing at home. My mouth gushed blood. It dripped down my chin onto the grass. One of my teeth had disappeared and the other became lodged in my gums. I remember screaming and running toward my dad. Dad took one look in my mouth and proceeded to search for my missing tooth. He never found it. Mom buckled me into the car and we rushed to see the pediatric dentist. I think I screeched a lot before the laughing gas set in. I hated my front teeth when they grew back in; they were awful, discolored, and in the wrong place. I wanted braces, but they weren't part of the plan. I have had plenty of other dental conundrums that needed to be cared for—root canals, crowns, and a number of cavities. I was blessed with bad teeth, so to speak. Eventually, my front teeth got a makeover, and it made my smile more confident. For years I hid my smile because I was ashamed of it, but I've learned to own my scar.

Moses, the famous Israelite leader had a scar, too. His scar was invisible: a stutter, which he didn't want God to use. He tried every excuse in the book to get out of leading God's people out of Egypt. God hates excuses. He told Moses, "Who has made man's mouth?" (Exodus 4:11-12, ESV). He went on to explain that He made both the mute and those who could talk. Who was Moses to say that he was useless?

I think a lot of times we feel the need to excuse ourselves from service because our disability is too great, or we aren't making enough of an impact, or we aren't important enough to start something. We want someone, anyone, to do it but us. Our scars can shape us from the inside out. We become wounded and construct a wall around ourselves to keep everyone and everything we don't consider safe out. Scars and wounds say a lot about us. They aren't always external; the internal ones can cause more psychological and mental damage. If we allow feelings of resentment reign in us, we not only hurt others, but we also hurt ourselves.

Joseph Stowell writes:

"When we encounter trouble, many of us find that our minds tend to get a little fuzzy, and that clear thinking eludes us. Trouble—especially over the long term—tends to confuse us and confound our thinking processes. However, we can take delight in the fact that in the midst of trouble there are some things we can always know; and the knowledge of those things enables us to count any trial or trouble a thing of joy."

Stowell doesn't say we should pretend we aren't hurting; rather, he explains:

"The word, 'consider' is borrowed from the accounting profession. It means to make a note of, to count, to consider, or to reckon on a ledger. It does not deal with how we feel, but with how we think and respond. It tells us that when trouble rocks our lives, something needs to be reckoned in our brains….The

one who "considers" is not concerned with changing the circumstances but with changing his or her attitudes and actions in the face of circumstances." [2]

In this stage, we have to draw columns and sort out the details, deciding where our reactions to our circumstances will fall. Our wounds and scars can fall into many different categories like revenge/bitterness, pity, blame, anger, and joy. If we are honest with ourselves, a number of our circumstances and scars fall into at least three of the first categories. But how many do we have in the category of joy?

I have been wounded by my front teeth. The thought of showing my teeth made me hide my smile for years. I didn't want to wear it. I was teased for it and I hated the way it looked. It wounded me that my parents couldn't afford braces to make my smile like everyone else's. I hated picture day at school. Every year, picture day made me want to crawl under a rock rather than let the photographer snap my photo. One year, he managed to make me laugh by telling me I resembled Jodi Sweeten from *Full House*. He told me I should ask for autographs. I thought that was hilarious! He asked me to say her trademark phrase "How rude!" and snapped my picture.

Do you have a scar that tells a story? Was it a positive or negative experience? Do you have someone you need to forgive for the wounds? Is that someone yourself? It is time to stop wounding yourself with the scars and walk with someone you trust: a friend, a counselor, a pastor, or loved one.

Moses didn't go alone; God let Moses' brother Aaron accompany him to Egypt, even though He was angry with Moses for making excuses:

"Is there not Aaron, your brother, the Levite? I know that he can speak well. Behold, he is coming out to meet you, and when he sees you, he will be glad in his heart. You shall speak to him and put the words in his mouth and I will be with your mouth and will teach you both what to do. He shall speak for you to the people, and he shall be your mouth, and you shall be as God to him. And take in your hand this staff, with which you shall do the signs." (Exodus 4: 14b-17, ESV)

God was working in both men to endure the hardships that would accompany them leaving Pharaoh's tyranny. God always went before them and never left them. Some people are still wounded, sharing the embittered battlements of their wounds, but others are shining in the stories of their scars. Let's help the walking wounded move toward a better stance, friends. No one should walk carrying their wounds alone.

---

[2] From the book *By The Dawn's Early Light*, Moody Publishers, 1990.

Activity 2: Scars and Wounds

We are going to share our scars. Pass out a new note card to each person. On the card, write down your scars: accidents, incidents, anything that has shaped you as a person. Pair off into groups of three and share your life scars.

Questions to consider: What do your scars say about you? How have they helped or hurt you as a person? Do they help you be more relatable to others?

Films for Discussion/Viewing

- On the Way to School

- Mury O'Shea was Here (aka: Inside I'm Dancing)

- Best Years of Our Lives

- My Left Foot

- Murderball

Examine the film. How does it add to or take away from our perceptions of those with a disability?

Spotlight: Kathryn Slagle, Epilepsy Advocate and Author, Kat's Temporal Lobe Diaries, Erie, PA

Kathryn Slagle is an author from Erie, PA with Temporal Lobe Epilepsy. Kathryn lives with mental illnesses of varying intensities, her husband, daughter, and son. She finds that writing helps her keep her emotions in check. She is committed to Epilepsy Awareness education. She has written for The Epilepsy Relay Blog, Living Well with Epilepsy as June's Person of the Month[3], and for Lucky Leaf magazine. When she isn't writing, she creates jewelry from glass, pottery, and other earthen materials.

Sample work from her flash fiction piece, "Let It Burn" can be found in the Appendix. Flash fiction is a piece of writing 1,000 words or less that gives the reader a fascinating story using vivid descriptions of characters, settings, and some awesome dialogue. You can read the entire piece at the end of this book in a section called Disability Writings. I hope you enjoy her work!

---

[3] If you are interested in Kathryn's story of life with epilepsy, see the Additional Information/Resources Section in the Appendix

Stage Three: Obstacles and Barriers - Seeing the Problems that Stand in the Way of Progress

It is possible to convey a wrong impression by repeating the exact words of someone else, to convey a lie by speaking the truth...

   ~Oswald Chambers, Our Ultimate Refuge

   I may be disabled physically, but I can still work.

   ~Inam Shaleati, TeleCare volunteer in Kentucky

I had a major problem: in class I couldn't concentrate on the coursework or lecture. I would sit through a class, but miss out on most of the material. I had no notes! I had to ask friends for copies of their notes. It didn't happen with every course. Some classes I simply understood better than others, like my Political Science course. Even there, I struggled with the professor's teaching method. He would put you on the spot to see if you were paying attention. I always felt embarrassed and ashamed because my lack of answers made it look like I wasn't listening. I always hoped the professor would not call on me. He knew the nature of my disability, but I knew I was still fair game for answering his questions. My professor was not a cruel person, nor was I asking to be treated like a snowflake. I am simply saying I had a big learning obstacle to overcome. I have simple frontal focal seizures. I look like I am daydreaming, but the truth is I am having a seizure. It happens so fast, like the blink of an eye. I knew I had a disadvantage; my brain had trouble focusing on classwork. I didn't want my seizures to excuse me from passing my classes, and I didn't want to be excluded from participating in class. I needed a note taker to aid in my class time.

In order to apply for a note taker, I had to undergo testing: a psychological evaluation to determine the strengths and weaknesses in how I process information. My previous neurologist wasn't exactly sure how my brain was affected by my epilepsy. He agreed that I needed to examine my brain's motor skills. This testing pushed me to my limits. If you ever get testing done, do not do it after taking midterms; you will sound like a jittery, unstable mess. That must have been what my psychiatrist thought as he gave me the exam. He had me undergo a series of rigorous tests, and I had trouble with a few of them. Admittedly, I am not a huge fan of IQ tests; they are difficult, and can make you seem like an imbecile or mentally unstable. In the end, he determined that I did indeed need a note taker. In addition to the psychological tests, I also had to send in documentation about my disability. Getting proper documentation is no easy feat. You have to apply and make sure the paperwork is sent correctly, as well as have a neurologist confirm your diagnosis. At that time, I had no neurologist. My neurologist had left, so it was a nurse practitioner that prescribed treatments for me. It was a disaster! I had to send in paperwork three times to get it authenticated by the psychologist who gave me the testing. Finally, after three weeks, I got the green light for accommodating my problem(s) in the classroom.

In II Kings 7:3-11, the author paints a devastating picture: four lepers residing outside their community. Lepers were social outcasts. If a leper were to step into a community, those who came into contact with him would be considered unclean. The Lord, though, does an incredible thing: He speaks through Elisha the prophet about delivering the people, Judah, from their enemies. He sends them out by scaring them. The lepers go into enemy territory the next morning, and "...when these lepers came to the edge of camp, they went into a tent and ate and drank..." They see a bounty of food, money, and resources. The lepers decide to share this good news with the people of their homeland, rather than hoarding it to themselves. Doesn't it seem strange to you that lepers, of any group of people, were used by God to deliver the news that the Syrians had left? If you were a citizen at the time, you would probably find it strange.

In I Kings 19:4-14, I recall the story of Elijah, Elisha's mentor. Elijah had just finished challenging the priests of Baal to a stand-off, successfully proving that the God of Judah was the true God with a blaze of fire that consumed the altar of Baal. Queen Jezebel was furious and sent men out to kill him. Elijah ran away and hid—first under a broom tree, then walking forty days to a cave far from Jezebel's clutches. Imagine doing something so powerful in the name of God and then having to run for your life. That would spoil your day, wouldn't it? Elijah became terrified and had an anxiety attack. He complained to God in verse 14 about being "very zealous for the Lord, the God of Hosts...and I, even I only, am left, and they seek my life, to take it away." But God reassured him of seven thousand faithful men who didn't bow down to Baal set aside to assist him. That's the problem with anxiety attacks: anxiety and fear can blow a situation out of proportion. It isolates us in our caves, distorting the truth of God and highlighting the harshness of our circumstances. Elijah did eventually leave his cave and return to his hometown. He couldn't stay in his cave forever; he had to face his problem head-on.

In the third phase, the disabled community faces a critical decision: will it play victim to the obstacles, or will it be a victor over the obstacles? The difference between these two positions is about a person's outlook. The victim sees only the obstacle, impossible, impenetrable, and impassable. The victim allows himself to be defined by the obstacle. Victims create barriers to keep others out. The victim becomes defeatist, thinking, "I am the only one with this problem. No one understands what I am going through." A victim can sink into depression and can become vindictive. A victor is the exact opposite. A victor greets challenges as opportunities for growth. A victor never lets an obstacle define him. A victor sees possibilities and fights to improve situations. Victors break down barriers to let people in. A victor never stops learning but keeps rising above adversity. A victor says, "I can do this; I am not alone. There is hope and help available." A victor may stumble and fall but will always rise again.

What barriers or obstacles are in your way? Are they self-made or are they formed by your environment? What steps can you take to help yourself move forward? Not every solution will work; sometimes, they take time and effort. It took seventy-five years for the first public vehicle to be accessible to everyone! It took eighty years for the first building to have handicap accessibility. If you feel like you've reached an impasse, don't lose heart. You are not alone; you are in good company with others who have hit the desert. Keep fighting and don't give up. Don't become a victim to your circumstances. Be a victor in the midst of them!

Activity 3: Breaking Barriers

Now we are going to break some barriers and face some obstacles. Split into groups of two and give out some disabilities: blindness, not using one arm, has a migraine, epilepsy. If one of the people in the group has a real-life disability, use that instead of one given by the leader. The disabled person must work with their partner to figure out how to be taken to a doctor's appointment, or someone who has a migraine needs to exit a room that has strobe lights or find a way to communicate their needs. After a few minutes, have them switch roles. Some of you will find this task extremely difficult, but I hope it challenges you to get creative and experience the world of those with a disability.

For those with a disability or those assigned one: how did it feel to be disabled? Did you find it easy or difficult to communicate your needs to your partner? For those of you in the role of caretaker: Did you find it easy or difficult to accommodate their needs? Were you able to communicate with your partner? How easy or difficult was it to work together? Why or why not? What did you learn from each other?

Films for Discussion/Viewing

- Frankenstein, Dracula, Wolfman, Dr. Jekyll and Mr. Hyde, Phantom of the Opera or Hunchback of Notre Dame (any year)

- Miracle Worker

- Forrest Gump

- Tiny Tim in Christmas Carol

- Soul Surfer

Examine the film. How does it add to or take away from our perceptions of those with a disability?

Spotlight: Inam Shaleati, TeleCare Volunteer Elder Service, Inc, Louisville, Kentucky

I know what it's like to need some help as a kid. And it gives me great joy to help others.

~Inam Shaleati

Inam Shaleati was born blind and diagnosed with cerebral palsy at six months old. Her home country, Syria, considered her cursed because of her birth defects, so her family moved to the United States when she was young to give her better opportunities. Since then, Inam has helped others in the Jefferson County community. She has won numerous volunteer awards including The Bell Award in 1999 and Hidden Heroes Award in 2013. She's helped with Radio Eye, a radio service program for those who are visually impaired or blind. She taught blind students at JCPS in Louisville, KY and has volunteered with Make-A-Wish Foundation and the local Cerebral Palsy organization. Over the years, Shaleati has lost many of her abilities and can no longer work long hours. She took up TeleCare, a nonprofit service to help people with disabilities age 50 and older to get living assistance over the phone as a way to support and stay connected with others. Inam offers some encouraging advice to those who have a disability:

"Be grateful for what you can do; be open minded to choosing other paths. Do what works best with your limitations, not solely in what you want to do. It is better than doing nothing. Ask what can be done. It is okay to do your best and try. You are given this one body. Handle it with care. It is okay to have a bad day. Don't be sad or angry all the time."

Inam offers further insight for those who want to connect better with the disabled, but don't know where to begin:

"If you see a disability, ask. Don't stare or think that person needs your help. If that person needs assistance, they will ask for it. Get positive with what they have and focus on what they can do."

Inam loves helping others with disabilities that are unable to care for themselves. She is both a passionate and compassionate person. Her voice vibrates with the boundless energy of her incredibly active schedule. You can find out more about the work she does in the Additional Resources/Information section of the Appendix.

Stage 4: Inclusion - Finding Accommodation and a Unique Voice

We all have a disability of some kind; all are lacking in one way or another. Saul has an injury to his leg. What if his personality was deformed? How much worse if his soul was lame? Preachers or teachers look for the good in all of us. (Bless them for doing so.) I don't see a cripple. I haven't met anyone yet who isn't handicapped in some way. So what's the big deal? Don't hide your deformity. Wear it like a Purple Heart.

~Georgiann Baldino[4]

2012 was the year I joined the Epilepsy Foundation of America. I had heard about it for a long time but was never a member. I forgot about it. Plenty of events happened between my time in college and working odd jobs. After various ailments and odd medical maladies, I joined the South Central/Western Pennsylvania chapter in Johnstown. I also joined another nonprofit called The Anita Kaufmann Foundation. It is a wonderful association which works to raise epilepsy awareness. The group had a service opportunity called Ambassadors of Purple, people who promote epilepsy education to their community. They help raise awareness through fundraisers, writing, teaching, and even art. I was fascinated and decided to join. The Coordinator of Ambassadors of Purple offered me some excellent advice on how to raise awareness and start a support group. My group doesn't have many members, but I love helping people work toward inclusion. I strive to integrate the disability experience into my community more and move toward belonging.

Inclusion is integrating a person into a community, church, or work setting by accommodating their needs. This includes: accessibility in buildings (push plates instead of opening doors, teletype machines, Braille on signs, closed captioning on screens, ramps), parking lots, vehicles, first aid training (heart attack, seizures, stroke, mental health crisis, suicide prevention), service animals, counseling, and support groups. When these things are in place, a person with a disability is no longer talked down to or looked upon as a liability. Rather, they are considered for a position and given responsibility for a task. Not every job is created equally, nor is every business trained to handle those who work "outside the box." Some jobs are too fast-paced, or employers are unwilling to mentor those with a disability. In 2013, I Want To Work, a government-sponsored partnership program, started an initiative to help young adults and adults with disabilities find employment suitable to their needs.

Inclusion starts when the able-bodied listen to the needs of the disabled. King David exemplifies integration in II Samuel 9. Here, he fulfills the promise he made to his best friend Jonathan in I Samuel 20, when he vowed to care for Jonathan and his family. When Jonathan was killed in battle, David was distraught. To fulfill his promise of showing mercy to the heirs of his best friend, David reached out to Mephibosheth, Jonathan's son who was crippled in his feet. While the story cannot confirm whether it was neurological (II Samuel 4:4 tells us that he was dropped by his nursemaid at five years old and became lame in both feet) or physical, Mephibosheth was a cripple for life. He had to rely on help from a servant named Ziba, who took him to see King David. I love Mephibosheth's reaction: "What is your servant, that you should show regard for a dead dog such as I?" (v 8b). In verse 13, it reads, "So Mephibosheth lived in Jerusalem and always ate at the king's table. For he was lame in both his feet." How awesome is that? King David gave a man, a crippled social outcast, the opportunity to dine at his table, raising him to the status of son and providing for his needs. He fulfilled his promise to his best

---

[4] American author, best known for writing historical fiction.

friend. This story brings us a challenge: how often are we willing to do that for other social outcasts in our community?.

What is so important about this story? It foreshadows something incredible that would happen centuries later in the form of Jesus Christ. Jesus would break social barriers, allowing lepers, women, Samaritans, tax collectors, and other outcasts (including those who had illnesses considered a curse by God) to join Him at the feast. He did more than simply let them eat; He let them belong, let them take part in something much more powerful. It was a life-changing experience that transformed them from the inside out—and was worth sharing with everyone!

I give you fair warning: at this stage, not everyone will want to include those who act outside of social norms. Some are afraid of conforming to a new standard. Some are scared that they will lose their rights. To me, I think the biggest thing people are terrified of, more than anything else, is change. Change is scary. Picture Linus van Pelt from the Peanuts comic strip, tightly clutching his security blanket. Some people are like that. Take away what makes them comfortable and they become erratic. Don't be afraid to go outside your comfort zone. Giving up your rights so others may live free is one of the most precious things you can do to help others. Giving up your right to yourself so God can use you is an even more difficult. Including those who are different and being willing to face your peers is tough. Admit it—our right to self is an obsession. Our culture is saturated with self-love, and time and again God warns us about the selfish nature of self. "Whoever would save his life will lose it, but whoever loses his life for my sake will find it" (Matthew 16:25, ESV).

How will you accommodate the needs of those who have a disability? Do you know of any place that is not accommodating? Is it someplace you can affect change, like in your workplace, school, or church? How will you better include those who are different from you? Remember the old song, "Jesus Loves the Little Children?" The first verse says, "Jesus loves the little children/all the children of the world/red and yellow, black and white/all are precious in His sight/ Jesus loves the little children of the world."[5] When did we stop believing that? Did the truth of it become too much? Let us take up that song again and believe that Jesus indeed loves "all the children of the world."

---

[5]Music by George Frederick Root and lyrics by Clare Herbert Woolston, 1864.

Activity 4: Inclusion

Now that you have communicated with someone different from you, it is time to take the next step and move toward inclusion. Decide on an activity that everyone can join in (a meal, a game night, movie night, etc). Invite those with a disability you have met. Make sure that person has a task to do. Make that person feel comfortable, important, and wanted.

Questions: Do you feel connected? Do you feel included? Does the person feel like he/she is a part of something? If not, what can you do to make sure that person feels included?

Films for Discussion/Viewing

- The Theory of Everything

- A Smile as Big as the Moon

- Parenthood

- Speechless

- Radio

- Monk

Questions: Examine the film; how does it add to or take away from our perceptions of those with a disability?

Spotlight: The Knepper Family, Kneppco, Somerset, PA

Rebecca Knepper was injured in a horseback riding accident in 2015. Her life changed when she found out she would never walk again. Her mom Jennie recalls, "No one knew the extent of her injuries. I had hope of what God would do. I never felt my daughter (Rebecca) would never walk again until months later. That is when it began to sink in."

Rebecca chimes in, "It was a gradual process. The biggest question was, "How do you adapt?"

For Rebecca, being in a wheelchair never felt like an obstacle, and her family views her disability as a benefit. The house's interior has a lift and a handicap accessible[6]bathroom for Rebecca's wheelchair. The living room was expanded and the outside of the house contains a ramp so Rebecca can easily move to one of her favorite places, the garden. Rebecca loves to read, draw, sew, cook, and play any of her various instruments. The most recent one she tried playing was the violin. This year, Rebecca started her own business on Pinterest to sell her home made artwork. [7]

Rebecca's positive attitude keeps her going, but it is more than simple hope. It is a deep-seated faith in God which keeps her focused. She offers some excellent, encouraging words to others who may face obstacles like hers:

"Stay positive in all situations. The first year is hard. You come to new places and new experiences in life. You learn to get through it; after a good amount of experience, things get easier. Sometimes, you may feel like you miss out on things, but you can find things to do and have friends do things with you."

Not a bad insight for a seventeen year old with a heart that keeps on growing!

---

6 For more information on how to make a house or building handicap accessible, see the Additional Information/Resources Section in the Appendix

7 If you want to check out her artwork, see the Additional Information/Resources Section in the Appendix

Stage Five: Belonging - Working Together As One Body

The problem we have with society is a real emphasis–and a quite right emphasis–on inclusion. I think at one level that's fine. However, inclusion is simply not enough. To include people in society is just to have them there. All we have to do is make the church accessible, have the right political structures, make sure people have a cup of tea at the end of the service or whatever. There is a big difference between inclusion and belonging.

To belong, you have to be missed. There's something really, really important about that. People need to long for you, to want you to be there. When you're not there, they should go looking for you. When things are wrong, people should be outraged – absolutely outraged that people are doing things against people with disabilities.

~John Swinton

I have not fully reached this stage. I am a work in progress when it comes to belonging. I can't tell you where I belong. I struggle to find my place in church every time I attend. Don't get me wrong: I love worshiping with my brothers and sisters on Sunday mornings, and I relish every chance I get to spend time with them. Yet I am always hungry, desiring more for my palate. I can't find it in my church. I can't confine it to a certain building or a certain space. Try as I might, I am always craving intimate time with people. The only time I can fully nourish that sense is when I am alone with God. It is not time with my friends that fills this void, though I have had some wonderful times with those who love Jesus. I can't fill my heart by any other means. It comes only when I have time with God.

If you ask me about finding a place to belong in church, I will stare blankly at you and say, "I don't know, do you have a space in mind?" A few may tell me to work with children or help teens, or perhaps suggest some other area of ministry in a sweet but condescending way to try to get rid of me. I have tried many of those pieces, but I am unable to fit in any of them. I believe God has called me to seek another route, one that He alone carved out for me. He has called me to be an advocate—to educate and assist others with disabilities. I use the word "called" rather than "ordained" or "taught." I have no professional experience as an advocate. Most of my training is from the hard knocks of my own life and from working with individuals like my brother who don't fit society's idea of "normal." I am attempting to educate people about the possibilities within the disabled in the body of Christ.

A great illustration for using others in the body of Christ is found in I Corinthians 12:22-25. Here, Paul discusses the diverse parts of the body.

"On the contrary, the parts of the body that seem to be weaker are indispensable, and on those parts of the body we think less honorable we bestow the greater honor, and our unpresentable parts are treated with greater modesty, which our more presentable parts do not require. But God has so composed the body, giving the greater honor to the part that lacked it, that there may be no division in the body, but that the members may have the same care for one another." (ESV)

What exactly are the hidden parts? The Bible doesn't provide any description. Could they include the disabled? Those with disabilities are often passed over as childish or incapable of performing higher tasks like taking a leadership role. Often in church, the disabled are placed in janitorial duties because it seems the best fit. We must remember that those with a disability provide a unique perspective of the world in Christ. Matthew 22:8-10 gives us a great illustration in the parable of the wedding feast. Here, Jesus discusses a king who had a big wedding party. He invited many people to join him in this great celebration, but a strange thing occurred: not one of his guests came. No one showed up for the party! Frustrated, the king extended the invitation to others: outsiders, outcasts, and nobodies who weren't considered well enough by society's standards (v 8-10). The king invited them and told them to dress up for the occasion. The guests come to enjoy the feast, for the most part. Only one is cast out for not following the king's decree. This story is a glorious tale of how God invites those who are not considered wise, beautiful, or good enough to belong at His grand party.

Somebody once asked me if I thought those with disabilities would ever truly belong in our society. I had to ponder the question a bit. Considering the broken, fragmented state of our world, I had to answer, "No." The world will never create an environment that fully encompasses a sense of belonging, no matter how many rules and regulations are put in place. Laws can enforce better treatment, education, or employment opportunities, however, the government cannot force a person to make friends with someone who is different. Church cannot do that perfectly, either. It can help foster belonging by creating good programs and becoming more inclusive in their services, but only God can reach the deepest longings of the heart. This is true for both those with disabilities and those without! The church provides the compass to find that belonging in Him. This can be accomplished when there are support groups, educational opportunities for growth, activities to promote social skills, and most importantly, training in how to better serve the disabled community. I hope we, as the body of Christ, can walk alongside those who have a disability and promote a more belonging place.

Where does your church, organization, or business fall when it comes to fostering interdependence and belonging? Does it listen to those who have a disability? Does it need to learn from those with a disability? How can you and your community better communicate with those who have a disability?

Activity 5: Belonging

Now that you have become acquainted with someone who is disabled, it is time to help them belong. Write a brief note to each person in the group, telling them what you like about them and what makes them special. After you finish, hand the notes to their recipients.

Questions: How did you feel after reading the notes from your classmates? Did it help to break down your fears or discomfort? Do you have any fears left? If so, what are they, and how can your classmates help you?

Films to Watch/Discuss

- Edward Scissorhands

- Finding Nemo

- First Do No Harm

- Temple Grandin

- Inside Out

- Not Dead Yet!

- Scorpion

- Born This Way

  Question: Examine the film; how does it add to or take away from our perceptions of those with a disability?

Spotlight: Mental Illness, Depression, and Suicide Prevention with Christian Welch, Spoken Word Poet, Ft. Lauderdale, FL

People say I'm the life of the party because I tell a joke or two

Although I make be laughing loud and hearty, deep inside I'm blue

So take a good look at my face

You'll see that my smile seems out of place

And if you look closer it's easy to trace the tracks of my tears

~Tracks of My Tears, Smokey Robinson[8]

Christian Welch is a spoken word poet who writes about his struggles with mental illness and those who have a mental illness. Christian writes, "I've been doing/writing poetry intently/doing spoken word for about 8 years now. I manage to get to tour/travel for poetry relatively often, thankfully so. My first tour was in September of 2014, but, about 4 to 5 years ago, I got more heavily involved in the music scene."

A native of Ft. Lauderdale, Florida, Welch expresses his perspectives on everything from mental illness to daily struggles in poetic form. His most popular piece, *Phone Calls at 3am* is also his most poignant piece. It offers help and hope to those who need a friend, whether they are experiencing PTSD or considering suicide. The statistics are high: 121 people die daily from suicide.[9] Welch teamed up with a nonprofit, Victims and Villains, to help spread the word about suicide prevention. *Phone Calls at 3am* is a wakeup call to the brokenness of the world, those who live in it, and those who live with it. You can read the full poem in the Disability Works section in the Appendix.

---

[8] 1963, Motown Records. Written by Smokey Robinson.

[9] Statistics, courtesy the American Foundation for Suicide Prevention. You can find them along with Christian Welch and Victims and Villains in the Additional Resources/Information Section in the Appendix..

Conclusion

If there was a country called disabled,
I would always have to remind myself that I am from there.

I often want to forget. I would have to remember...to remember.

In my life's journey I am making myself

At home in my country.

~Disabled Country by Neil Marcus[10]

My journey as an advocate continues to take shape. My brother has had a significant impact on my choice to advocate for the disabled. The movie theater story is a great example of my life being turned upside down. Initially, it seemed as if I were the only kid with a unique brother, but as I grew there were countless others who could say, "I have similar experiences to yours. I can relate to knowing and loving someone outside "normal."" One of the biggest devices I have utilized is humor. Humor and plenty of laughs keep my life being anything but commonplace.

I'm on a roller coaster ride of adventures, and the dips and turns have enhanced my life. From diagnosis to development of my skills, epilepsy is a tour de force of stages. A disability changes you, wrecking your equations for the perfect life. You can't add, subtract, multiply, or divide your time into idyllic proportions. A disability reconfigures that formula, often against your best intentions. It is important to not shirk off the response to it or to regard it lightly as another phase of life. It is important to walk through every stage toward reaching an interdependent life together. No one needs to do this alone.

From Isolation, Scars and Wounds, Problems and Barriers, Inclusion, and someday to fully Belonging, I have experienced all these stages at some point. Sometimes, I went back and forth between stages like a ping pong ball. I can't say my experience of these stages is similar to others in disabled community. Some people take these steps at a slower pace, or a faster one. Some take months or even years to walk through them completely. As I go through another year on this highway, I continue to develop my skills and help other people walk the discouraging pathways. Whatever the pace, we need to work together. Let us consider what Paul commands us to do and walk these paths together, encouraging each other as we create a more belonging place.

---

[10] Poet, disabilities advocate. See the Appendix for Additional Resources to find his piece in the collection.

APPENDIX

Introduction, Appendix: Defining Disability

Over the decades, the definition of a disability has evolved from a disability-first to a person-first language. Each activist movement has brought a new perspective on how to address a disability. Of course, points of contention remain. The biggest problem is defining the person who has a disability. Not everyone views a disability as hidden; rather, it is more a visible thing. Some see the disability only and forget about the person behind the disability; others want to see the person first, disability second. It all depends on different factors: social environment, culture, and background. If a person grew up in a nurturing, supportive environment, then the disability comes secondary. If the culture and environment emphasizes the disability as cumbersome, a burden, or a curse, then the disability comes first and the person second. In our nation, there is a half-and-half balance between disability-first and person-first perspective. While not everyone agrees on the best way to describe a person who has a disability, there is plenty of room for progress. If you want to read the entire classification system on disabilities, *The Huffington Post* did an excellent opinion piece on the semantics behind disability. You can see it in the Resources section of this book.

Additional Resources/Information

- American Foundation for Suicide Prevention: https://www.afsp.org
- Accessible House Plans Resource: https://www.houseplanresource.com/plans/accessible-house-plans
- Action Fund article: https://actionfund.org/images/nfb/publications/fr/fr22/fr06sum22.htm
- Disabled Country service page: https://www.disabledcountry.com/about#!
- "Disabled Country" You Tube Video link: https://www.youtube.com/watch?v=Z4JrWZljatw
- Elder Service Article: https://elderserveinc.org/ceo-letter-summer-2017/
- "Epilepsy". *The Huffington Post.* http://www.huffingtonpost.ca/epilepsy-ontario/epilepsy_b_5591039.html
- Epilepsy Foundation of America: https://www.epilepsy.com
- Evel Janelle Facebook page: https://www.facebook.com/onefungal/
- How to Make Your Home Accessible: https://www.disabled-world.com/disability/accessibiltiy/homes/
- Rebecca Knepper's Pinterest page: https://www.pinterest.com/beccaknepp/
- Inam Shaleati, Telecare volunteer: Hidden Heroes article: http://www.wdrb.com/story/23843161/wdrb-hidden-hero-she-wont-stop-giving
- Kathryn Slagle, Living Well with Epilepsy Article: https://www.livingwellwithepilepsy.com/portfolio/june-6-kathrynslagle/
- Victims and Villains on Facebook: https://www.facebook.com/victimsandvillains.
- Christian Welch, spoken word poet Facebook page: https://www.facebook.com/killthepoetsrebel

Myths and Misnomers about Disabilities

- Vengeful, angry because of disability
- Super disability - have extraordinary senses like Superman or the Incredible Hulk
- Pitiable creature, charity case
    - Tiny Tim Syndrome
    - Mad genius that is locked away
    - Dr. Frankenstein Effect
- Deaf people can read lips
- Blind people have to touch faces
- Epilepsy is always a fall-on-the-floor, foam-at-the-mouth, shake-all-over experience
- Ends life to stop being a burden on others
- Blissfully innocent or demonic in nature
- Imparts wisdom to another before dying
- Is curable
- Is a holy innocent
- Can't do anything without an able-bodied person to "guide" them
- Can't be in a relationship of any kind
  Can you think of any other myths that exist?

A scene from "The Best Years of Our Lives" with Oscar Winner Harold Russell (former Legionnaire and real-life amputee) and Teresa Wright as Homer and his sweetheart, Wilma. Image courtesy, 20ᵗʰ Century Fox.

Inside Hollywood: Disability Drama

In the late 1930s and early 1940s, a new style of film showed up in theaters. In this new genre, the plot focused on characters facing tremendous obstacles, whether through disfigurement or a terrible accident. These characters would either overcome or die from it. This genre would be become known as **Disability Drama**. In a typical disability drama, the characters are thrust into an incident which causes a drastic shift in circumstances. Sometimes, the character is miraculously healed; other times, the character is a martyr and dies terribly. One of the most well-known films to feature a disability is the film *The Best Years of Our Lives*. In this picture, three soldiers return from World War II and attempt to reintegrate into their hometown. Homer, one of the main characters, lost his hands in battle and has to adjust to life with hooks for hands. His girlfriend Wilma doesn't care that his hands are hooks and still wants to marry him. He is not the only one facing major obstacles. His friend has post-traumatic stress disorder (which was unknown at the time, but the painful side effects are showed acutely in the film), and their associate can't reconnect with his grown children or to his new job at a bank. The film scored three Oscars—Freddie March won for Best Leading Actor, Best Picture for 1946, and Best Director, William Wyler. *The Best Years of Our Lives* set the standard for production of disability dramas. It became the first film in which an actor with a disability, Harold Russell for Best Supporting Actor, won his or her own Academy Award. No disabled actor before then—and, sadly, no one since then (with the exception of Marlee Matlin)—has won an Academy Award. *The Best Years of Our Lives* paved the way for actors with disabilities to take on more serious, dramatic roles.

Disability Films and Programs for All Ages

For Families: Rated G and PG

Finding Nemo *Frozen *Shrek Films (1,2, 3, and 4) *Wreck-It Ralph *How To Train Your Dragon(1 and 2) *Cars *A Dolphin's Tale (1 and 2) *Finding Dory *Alice in Wonderland (both the animated version as well as the live-action film made in London by Hallmark) *Wizard of Oz *Christmas Carol *Edward Scissorhands (may be a little scary, so parents, please accompany children when watching) *Smile as Big as the Moon *The Best Years of Our Lives *Miracle Worker (parents, please be ready to answer questions; some of the material may be difficult to grasp, but it is a good film to watch with kids) *Balto *Sing! *Inside Out *Horse Whisperer

Teens and Adults: Rated PG-13 and R

Phantom of the Opera *Frankenstein *Dr. Jekyll and Mr. Hyde *the Invisible Man *Dracula *Forrest Gump *The Theory of Everything *The Fault in Our Stars *Electricity *My Left Foot *Fifty First Dates *What About Bob? *I Am Sam *Radio *Still Alice *A Beautiful Mind *Shadowlands *Ray *A Child is Waiting (has outdated language that may be difficult to understand; if you watch it, stick with it and don't get discouraged!) *Garden State *To Kill A Mockingbird *Freaks (a controversial film critics love or loathe; it's important to include here because of its portrayal of disabilities) *Temple Grandin *First Do No Harm *Gojira(Godzilla) *Simon Birch

Documentaries (unrated)

On The Way to School *Murderball *Rory O'Shea (Inside I'm Dancing) *Not Dead Yet! *Autism the Musical *A is for Autism

Television Shows for Viewing and Discussing (Reality, Drama, Comedy)

The United States of Tara *Monk *Life Goes On *Scorpion *Born This Way *Speechless *House *Glee *Ironside *Little People, Big World*Bones *The Incredible Hulk (Lou Ferrigno, who plays The Incredible Hulk, is deaf) *Switched At Birth (if you decide to view this program, focus on the episode where the characters speak with American Sign Language the entire episode) *Degrassi *Degrassi High *Alphas *Heroes *Heroes: Reborn

*This is a sampling of films and shows which feature characters that have a disability. For a more complete list, check out Disabled World's website: www.disabledworld.com or IRIS, a part of the Disabled World's film collaboration project. It is a well-documented preservation of film, TV, and documentary history: https://www.irisproject.org

Disability Stories and Poetry

Let It Burn by Kat Slagle

Tillie stood and watched the house burn as the lava flow finally overtook it. Everyone knew it was coming for months. It was still not enough time to plan for a disaster in slow motion. It was too late now. The disaster was here and there was nothing to do what watch. She was in no personal danger. She could walk away from the lava. Nothing else could.

The greedy lava had been eating up everything in its path since June. Standing on the edge of November it was nearly a relief to have it here already. The anxiety has come to a head. No more worrying about what may happen. It has happened. The house was burning.

It felt like they were in an oven. The heat was inescapable, the lava just kept on coming and coming. It took down everything in its wake. Entire trees and forests were gone. The lava had overtaken the Buddhist Cemetery yesterday. The cemetery was completely gone. Where was she supposed to go to mourn her father's bones now? They were less than dust now.

She knew the risk when she bought the house. They had to sign the Lava Flow clause and buy the extra insurance. She knew, but never really thought it would happen. Kali Ma always kept the lava flow to the south, why would it go north? The risk seemed worth the reward. It *was* an island paradise. The sheer lack of snow made the lava in the south seem like a minor annoyance. Less troublesome than a mosquito. Until the lava flow changed. Nobody knows why. Not even the volcanologist who live in Hawaii and monitor the volcanoes 26 hours a day. The lava came North.

Now the officials were allowing Tillie to stay outside a barricade and watch her home go up in flames. The unceasing lava just kept coming, a writhing mass of black and red destruction. The fire wouldn't spread; the lava was just going to eat that too. The smoke billowed out of the mouth of the dragon.

She thought about the amount of time it would take for this lava flow to finish its run to the sea. How long until the Earth reclaims the newfound ground and turns it to soil and land. Eons. It will be eons before someone will live here again. Everybody wondered if the town could be saved. Tillie's house wouldn't be. The lava was coming and it was unpredictable. Nobody knew what exactly would burn until it did. One arm of the flow might peter out and another grows angry and molten red.

There was a stark contrast of the shiny, black, obsidian cooling lava on top and the radioactive red, killer lava that kept pouring out of the black at the inconceivable temperature of 2000 degrees

The ooze moved with deliberation. "The Flow is gonna do what the Flow is gonna do." It became the town's mantra. At least the waiting was almost over. The house was ablaze and would soon be gone. It would burn to the ground and be overtaken by the lava beast. You wouldn't know there was ever a house there.

Tillie finished her cigarette and tossed it towards the inferno. Too late to worry about litter now. Too late to worry about anything that she left behind that she couldn't carry or wasn't looted. That was all gone now. The dragon would eat that too.

You can't stop the lava. It's not a hurricane you can pray pass and eventually the eye of the storm will blow off to somewhere else. You can't hope the snow won't fall. Earthquakes stop. Lava laughs at you. You can just stand there and watch it burn. It was the ugliest thing she'd ever seen. It was hypnotic. The lava was ugly and beautiful and destructive and making new land from the depth of the Earth. These Hawaiian volcanoes are working volcanoes. They make islands. The lava is eating up the village, but the island will be bigger because of it. Such a paradox within a disaster. Nobody knows where the flow is going to go.

Tillie knows. The lava will destroy her. Her waiting is over. There is a kind of relief wrapped in her grief.

Phone Calls at 3 am by Christian Welch

I understand, often times, that the last thing that we want to hear at 3 am in the morning is honesty, but if you open up to me I'll be honest with you, because your car is gone;
or your girlfriend is, again.
Maybe you didn't have enough money for alcohol, maybe you had too much.
Maybe someone passed you like a secret through their hands and that's why you are so quiet,
or you shake up every night,
your body jammed like a magazine, trying to manage this PTSD that we've seen slipping through you,
post-mortar spark show, you can't clean of the shrapnel when it's dug this deep,
or you keep seeing your dead relatives, or you delve into self-prophetic cannibalization,
whatever is eating away at you...
Listen, and let it click into the spindles turning darkness throughout the vessel of your heart,
your body may be a city in ruins but it is never too late to start rebuilding.
Stop hanging from your own halo, a train of highways wrapped around your collar bones and back,
have you ever seen a palace made out of glass gears rising up out of red dust?
I can see one shatter in the liquid of your eyes every time someone respects you enough to look into them,
they are so beautiful, but you would not know that because you have not seen your reflection in months,
your skin is a cabin that you feverishly scrub dust in,
you've become a pale person, full of ghosts;
full of midnight things, and you allow yourself to believe that you can see better with your hands covering your eyes,
I understand...
That in a world, so polluted, it is hard to feel at home because we cannot look up at night into the faded photographs of who we used to be,
but your body is something that God poured Himself out to create;
He held out a hand to catch the thought, kept the blood splatter, and what we're stuck with is that matter of factly, you are not of any man's creation,
so break the highways out of your halos and do not let any construct of him be the death of you.
I understand, that when we opened those eighth grade note passes, they never said yes, but one day,
ticker tape love poems will fall from the sky through the honey of your lips and someone will kiss you as
your heart drops into the zero of your stomach turning over inside of itself, you are only you,
so stop using the excuse that you weren't yourself,
because you can only be what you are,
I'm not married.
I've spent a lot of my life with a lot of anger and disdain inside of my heart because I see the dirt that my, and your lungs are rot through with,
I've not looked into my mirror for months on end, end even when I did, it was for all of the wrong

reasons,

I've turned my back on myself, and far more on God, in ways that I never thought I would have,

and I've done disgusting things, disgusting things, to people who let me love them, both, like a slow dance and a mosh pit,

I woke up to demons once;

but I hope you hear this through the static collapsing against your shaken bones,

I just want to tell you my body; I want to tell you that this is what a temple looks like;

when you place your hands onto your chest, say "This is what a temple feels like.";

when at home, and most lonely, place your hand to where your heart pushes hardly through to the surface,

and listen.

This is a song that God places inside of our mouths.

When your hands are in front of you, see them, know, that these are a way to make beautiful things out of all that you touch.

Knowledge of the word of God, your Father, is a spark,

your mind is a lamp,

your eyes are lanterns,

that you hang inside of your body,

my ex-fiancé still has reasons to smile;

my eyes are oceans,

the poor in spirit will one day be blessed;

those who mourn will laugh,

there is someone who would come to me on an interstate at midnight and try to push my car out of a ditch,

I woke up today,

I am not attributed with the person that I was;

and God said "let Us make man in Our image;".

These are some of the most beautiful things that I know.

That I will ever know.

Medical History that Helped Change Our Perception of Disabilities

- Hippocrates - physician and father of medicine, father of epilepsy research (4000 B.C.) Wrote a book called *On the Sacred Disease,* in which he debunks the myth that disabilities such as epilepsy are a curse from the gods/goddesses. "It is thus with regard to the disease called Sacred: it appears to me to be nowise more divine nor more sacred than other diseases, but has a natural cause from the originates like other affections. Men regard its nature and cause as divine from ignorance and wonder, because it is not at all like to other diseases." ~Hippocrates, *On The Sacred Disease* as translated by Francis Adams

- Philippe Pinel (1745-1826) - leading French psychiatrist. Reclassified the mentally ill as diseased rather than immoral. Broke the chains off the mentally ill at the Bicêtre Asylum and later in Salpêtrière Asylum. Classified mental illnesses, pioneered individual case studies, systematic record keeping, and vocational training.

- Jean Marc Gaspard Itard (1774-1838) - student of Pinel. Discovered Victor, the Wild Boy of Averyon. Victor was his subject for the idea of the "blank slate." He trained Victor to eat, speak, dress himself, sleep in a bed, and eat cooked food, to name a few things. Itard found a simple means of communication between him and Victor. Victor made great strides, but not to the extent Itard hoped for; he wanted Victor to become "super" normal. He did prove that those who had severe mental illnesses could be trained to learn new tasks to a certain extent.

- 1775 - Virginia establishes first hospital to treat "idiots, lunatics and other people of unsound mind."

- 1812 - Benjamin Rush, the father of American psychiatry, writes his book *Observations and Inquiries upon the Diseased Mind.* First psychiatry textbook in the U.S. He was a signer of the Declaration of Independence.

- Jean-Étienne Dominique Esquirol (1782-1840) - student of Pinel. Famous French psychiatrist. His book, *Des Maladies Mentales*, was published in 1838. In it, he divided intellect into two levels: imbecility and idiocy. Imbeciles were nearly normal while idiots were considered without proper function of the senses. Though terribly flawed, it did influence the classification of disabilities.

- Dorothea Dix (1802-1887) - advocate and teacher from Massachusetts. Pushed for better care for those with all disabilities. In a speech to Congress presented by her friend and social reformer, Dr. Samuel Gridley Howe, she wrote the following in 1848: "More than nine-thousand idiots, epileptics, and insane in these United States, destitute of appropriate care and protection. Bound with galling chains, bowed beneath fetters and heavy iron balls, attached to drag-chains, lacerated with ropes, scourged with rods, and terrified beneath storms of profane execrations and cruel blows; now subject to jibes, and scorn, and torturing tricks, now abandoned to the most loathsome necessities or subject to the vilest and most outrageous violations." Though President Pierce vetoed the act to clean up the institutions, her passionate appeals paved the way for better care to come in the next decade.

- Édouard Séguin (1812-1880) - director and physician at Salpêtrière Asylum in France. Created a school for the mentally ill. Believed that mental illness was caused by a deficiency in the nervous and motor systems. Developed a physiological method to help increase motor and sensory function.

- Maria Montessori (1870-1950) - developed the first training school in the United States for those with mental and physical disabilities.

- Dr. Samuel Gridley Howe (1801-1876) - social reformer, and director of the Perkins School for the Blind. He established the Massachusetts School for Idiotic and Feeble-Minded Youth, an experimental boarding school in South Boston for youth with intellectual deficiencies. Both Seguin and Howe firmly believed in the importance of family and community, and wanted their schools to prepare children with disabilities to live with the rest of society. Led to an increase of special training schools along the East Coast in 1857. By 1866, the effects of the war closed many of his special schools.

- Dr. William Little (1810-1894) - British surgeon, discovers Cerebral Palsy (first named Little's Disease) in 1860.

- Dr. Jonathan Langdon Down (1828-1896) - published his findings on what is now known as Down Syndrome in 1866.

- 1869 - the first wheelchair patent registered in U.S. patent office

- June 7, 1876 - the Medical Association for Mental Illness is formed. Members include Édouard Séguin, Hervey B. Wilbur, G.A. Doran, C.T. Wilbur, H. Knight, and Isaac Kerlin as the six superintendents. They meet in Medina, Pennsylvania to discuss treatments, managing, causes, and statistics for those who have a mental illness.

- 1883 - Sir Francis Galton coined the term "eugenics"; promoted the idea that intelligent, well-bred people produce children, not those of lower intellect. Lower intellectual people would produce race degeneration, responsible for the social ills. His idea was to sterilize those with disabilities.

- 1927 - Harvard medical researchers Philip Drinker and Louis Agassiz Shaw develop the first Iron Lung used to treat polio.

- 1943 - Dr. Leo Kanner of Johns Hopkins Medical University introduces the classification of autism in his paper, "The Nervous Child."

- 1948 - Albert Deutsch writes *Shame of the States*, a photographic expose on New York's Letchworth Village, an institution for the disabled. Exposes awful living conditions. Coins the phrase, "euthanasia through neglect" in regard to those who have a disability and are put away from society.

- 1952 - Dr. Jonas Salk develops the polio vaccine.

- 1953 - 100 boys are subjected to testing at The Fernand School in Waverly, Massachusetts to see the effects of radiation in food on people.

- 1954 - Philip Roos, Executive Director of NARC (National Alliance of Retarded Children), psychiatrist, and parent coins the term, "deaf ear syndrome," defined as what happens when professionals don't listen to parents or people who have a disability. The professional would often provide outdated bits of medical wisdom which were unfit for the situation.

- 1955 - Representative John Fogarty, a health expert, gathered the medical association heads to discuss better options for families and individuals with disabilities.

- 1961 - Dr. Robert Guthrie's PKU screening test is ready to be implemented.

- 1963 - New polio vaccine created by Dr. Albert Sabin. Taken orally instead of by syringe.

- Dr. Bengt Nirje, Erik Bank-Mikkelsen, and Karl Grunewald establish the Normalization Principle. Normalization consists of making life for a person with mental illnesses' day as routine as possible. Was put into law and included in the President's Panel for Mental Illness discussion in 1969. Dr. Wolf Wolfensberger would later expand this concept and write about "social role valorization," which discussed how stereotypes and stigmas clouded society's perception of people with disabilities.

- 1970 - Dr. Elizabeth Boggs and Dr. Elsie Helsel work on Developmental Disabilities Services and Facilities Construction Amendments

- 1980 - Charlotte Des Jardins writes book, *How to Organize an Effective Parent/Advocacy Group and Move Bureaucracies.* Lays out steps in making waves for change.

- 1992 - Dr. Ben Carson, a young medical student, perfects a neurological surgery to help those who need brain surgery. It is less invasive and dangerous.

- 2017 - A recent test developed in Switzerland studies effects of virtual reality on those confronting their fears versus face to face confrontation of fears. Discovered that fears confronted in virtual reality as effective as those faced in person.

Laws that Moved Advocacy Forward/Changed History

- Brown v. Board of Education
  - Did more than desegregate for students of color; it helped desegregate for those with disabilities as well
- The Rehabilitation Act of 1973
  - Equal opportunities for individuals with disabilities produced by the federal government to act on their behalf for affirmative action
- Individuals with Disabilities Education Act of 1975
  - Ensures services to children with disabilities, including early intervention services and educational opportunities.
  - Not all schools are able to provide services, especially in the private sector (a crisis which continues today)
- Urban Architectural Barriers Act 1968 - public buildings (schools, offices, restaurants, hotels, doctor's offices, hospitals), must be wheelchair accessible
- Urban Mass Transit Act of 1970 - all vehicles are required to have wheelchair lifts. Unfortunately, implementation was delayed for twenty years.
- 1971 - Wyatt v. Stickney - those with mental or physical disabilities no longer to be locked away in institutions; they are to receive education and proper treatment
- 1972 - PARC v. Pennsylvania - no longer denies those with physical or mental disabilities from public education
  - Lead to passage of Education for All Handicapped Children Act of 1975
- 1980 - Civil Rights of Institutionalized Persons Act - fought for rights of those who are put in institutions that are being abused, violated or neglected.
- Baby Doe Squads created in 1981 after the family of Baby Doe is denied life-saving surgery for their son, who has Down Syndrome
- Telecommunications for those with Disabilities Act makes telecommunications devices available in public buildings for those who are blind, deaf, and/or hard of hearing
- The Americans with Disability Act - 1990
  - Law created by Tony Coehlo and Bob Dole
  - No person with a disability is denied a job on the basis of his or her disability
  - Make buildings, vehicles, and restrooms handicap accessible
  - Cannot deny a person a pass on train, plane or bus
  - But not everyone is on board with it – there are still loopholes and the law isn't perfect (see 1999 court case)
- 1993 - Holland v. Sacramento City Unified School District verifies rights of students with disabilities to attend school with nondisabled children
- 1995 - "When Billy Broke His Head…and other tales of Wonder" premiers on PBS. Gives viewers a look into the world of disabilities and the disability rights movement
- Helen L. v. Snider - landmark case to allow those who have a disability to not be placed in a nursing home but have the option of home health care
- 1996 - Not Dead Yet organized to counteract the actions of Dr. Kevorkian and the right to die movement. Preventing the Do Not Resuscitate on those with severe mental disabilities and pushing them out of the way of schools, hospitals and nursing homes

- 1999 - Three Supreme Court Cases rule in reversal of the ADA; ruling proves that those who have hidden disabilities like diabetes and epilepsy are not necessarily protected against discrimination. Disability advocates protest the ruling and fight for clarification on the ADA
- 2005 - Not Dead Yet protests the neglect and removal of a feeding tube from Terri Schavo. While Schavo never indicated a DNR order or a living will, she ended up dying from starvation and neglect.
- 2008 - Disabilities and Media Alliance Project is born
- The ADA revised the Equal Employment Opportunity Policy in 2010
  - Included the Don't Ask Don't Tell policy - prospective employees do not have to share the nature of his/her disability. They also don't have to ask for medical information about the disability unless it is required for the job. This often creates more problems than solutions. How can a business better accommodate to the needs of workers with disabilities if the prospective employee won't talk about it?

*For more information, check out the Disability History website, https://www.yodisabled.org.

Historical Images

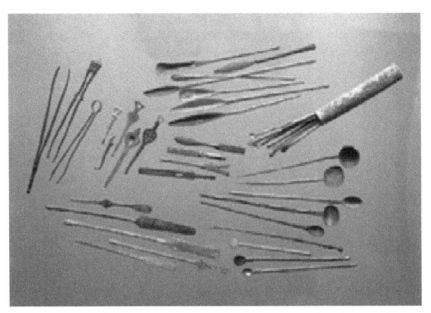

Medical Devices dating back 4000 BC, Jerusalem; these tools were used to help treat various ailments including those in the brain. Image courtesy, Biblical Archeology Society. www.biblicalarchaeology.org

Sample poster of how mental illness was seen back in the early 1920s. After the scare of immigration, mental illness bore the brunt of crime and social stigmas. The idea would be popularized in a book called *The Kallikak Family,* a bestseller for the time. Image, courtesy The Minnesota Government Developmental Disabilities Department.

From the 1933 horror classic, *The Wolfman of London*, starring Henry Hull and Valerie Hobson. This motion picture vocalized the fears and phobias of those who had mental health and physical disabilities. The monster movies of this time made them seem as mad as Dr. Frankenstein. Many great actors emerged from genre including Sir Christopher Lee, Vincent Price and Bela Lugosi. Image, courtesy Twentieth Century Fox.

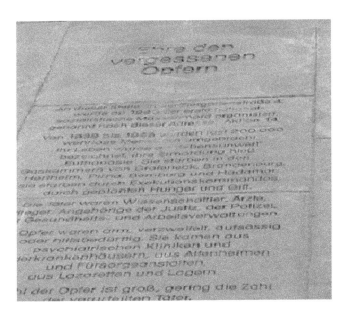

Memorial to remember those who died first in the Holocaust: the disabled were among the earliest deaths in concentration camps. Feared by Hitler and other Nazi supporters, this was eugenics in practice. The memorial is found in Oppenheim, Germany.

This sample image shows a person in a wheelchair unable to get down on the sidewalk. Back then, it was legal to ban those with a disability from public places, including the sidewalk. Image, courtesy of the Everybody Exhibit, History of Disabilities at the Smithsonian in Washington, DC

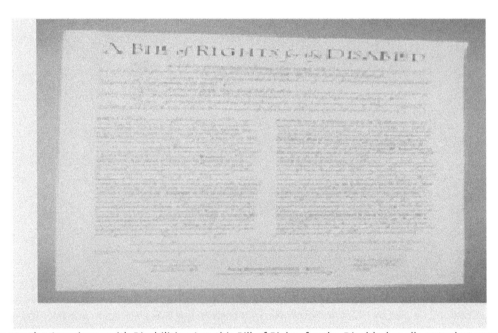

Precursor to the Americans with Disabilities Act, this Bill of Rights for the Disabled spells out what people with disabilities are allowed to do under the Constitution of the United States. Image from the Albert Einstein College of Medicine of Yeshiva University in New York.

ADAPT disability rights activists protest in 1990. Image, Smithsonian's EveryBody exhibit.

To Justin Dart.   without your drive, your
'believing' and your leadership this day would not have
been possible. With respect + friendship Gg Bush

Signing of The Americans with Disabilities Act (ADA), 1990. Autographed picture of President George H.W. Bush with disability activists Evan Kempe, left and Justin Dart, right. Image, courtesy Smithsonian EveryBody Exhibit.

CPSIA information can be obtained
at www.ICGtesting.com
Printed in the USA
LVHW101415120219
607105LV00034BA/525/P